Don't Quit Your Daydream

DON'T QUIT YOUR DAYDREAM

Copyright © Summersdale Publishers Ltd, 2019

Text by Peggy Jones and Sophie Martin

All rights reserved.

No part of this book may be reproduced by any means, nor transmitted, nor translated into a machine language, without the written permission of the publishers.

Condition of Sale
This book is sold subject to the condition that it shall not, by way of trade or otherwise, be lent, resold, hired out or otherwise circulated in any form of binding or cover other than that in which it is published and without a similar condition including this condition being imposed on the subsequent purchaser.

An Hachette UK Company
www.hachette.co.uk

Summersdale Publishers Ltd
Part of Octopus Publishing Group Limited
Carmelite House
50 Victoria Embankment
LONDON
EC4Y 0DZ
UK

www.summersdale.com

Printed and bound in China

ISBN: 978-1-78685-797-2

Substantial discounts on bulk quantities of Summersdale books are available to corporations, professional associations and other organizations. For details contact general enquiries: telephone: +44 (0) 1243 771107 or email: enquiries@summersdale.com.

Don't Quit Your Daydream

summersdale

INTRODUCTION

As children, we spent our days imagining the impossible, creating the fantastical and finding the incredible in the most ordinary things. But why should this innocent and pure way of living be off limits to adults? A little fun and imagination never hurt anyone. And sometimes the best way to deal with everyday life is to escape it, if just for a moment or two.

This little book offers ideas and inspiration on how to embrace your free spirit and find magic wherever you go and whatever you do. So what are you waiting for? It's time to say yes to escaping the mundane, rediscovering your inner child and, most importantly, following your daydreams.

SPLASH AROUND IN PUDDLES.

GO CLOUD SPOTTING.

MIX A LITTLE FOOLISHNESS
WITH YOUR SERIOUS PLANS.
IT'S LOVELY TO BE SILLY AT
THE RIGHT MOMENT.

Horace

CLIMB A TREE.

PLAY YOUR FAVOURITE CHILDHOOD VIDEO GAME, INVENT STORIES ABOUT THE PEOPLE WHO PASS YOU ON THE STREET, MAKE A TIME CAPSULE.

They who dream by day are cognizant of many things which escape those who dream only by night.

Edgar Allan Poe

Make the most decadent luxury hot chocolate.

WOOL-GATHERING, *n.* INDULGENCE IN AIMLESS THOUGHT OR DREAMY IMAGINING.

REREAD A FAVOURITE CHILDHOOD BOOK.

BUILD A BLANKET FORT,
INVITE FRIENDS
OVER FOR A SLEEPOVER,
DRAW THE VIEW
FROM YOUR WINDOW,
POST A LETTER
TO ONE OF YOUR
NEAREST AND DEAREST,
HAVE AN INDOOR
PICNIC ON A
RAINY DAY.

A HEART WITHOUT DREAMS IS LIKE A BIRD WITHOUT FEATHERS.

Suzy Kassem

PRETEND YOU ARE SOMEONE ELSE FOR A DAY.

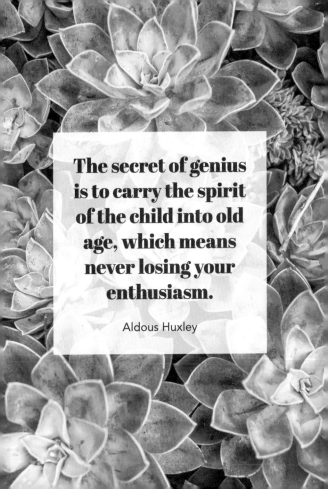

The secret of genius is to carry the spirit of the child into old age, which means never losing your enthusiasm.

Aldous Huxley

SING ALONG TO YOUR FAVOURITE ALBUM AT FULL VOLUME.

CREATE A SCRAPBOOK OF YOUR

FAVOURITE

THINGS, GO TO THE

SEASIDE,

CATCH A BUS TO

SOMEWHERE NEW.

LIVING

THE

DREAM.

MAKE A FINGERPRINT PAINTING.

GO STARGAZING.

Do not wait; the time will never be "just right".

NAPOLEON HILL

FINISH A JIGSAW PUZZLE, LEARN HOW TO DO A **HEADSTAND**, TEACH YOURSELF PIG LATIN, EAT WITH YOUR FINGERS, CONCENTRATE ON SMELLS, **FEELINGS**, SIGHTS AND NOISES YOU WOULD USUALLY IGNORE.

**NOTHING HAPPENS
UNLESS FIRST WE DREAM.**

Carl Sandburg

Find treasures in your local second-hand store.

Embrace the
glorious mess
that you are.

Elizabeth Gilbert

YOUR LIFE IS WHAT YOU MAKE IT.

PULL A SILLY FACE WHENEVER YOU PASS A SECURITY CAMERA, EAT A DOUGHNUT WITHOUT LICKING YOUR LIPS, LEARN A DANCE ROUTINE TO A CHEESY POP SONG.

PRETEND TO BE A STATUE IN A BUSY SHOPPING MALL.

START A DREAM JOURNAL.

If a little dreaming is dangerous, the cure for it is not to dream less but to dream more, to dream all the time.

Marcel Proust

Hula-hoop to music.

THRIVE, *v.* PROSPER;
FLOURISH.

BLOW BUBBLES, **TOAST** MARSHMALLOWS, WRITE A FICTIONAL STORY BASED ON **YOUR DAY,** HAVE A WATER FIGHT, GO FORAGING.

START A PODCAST.

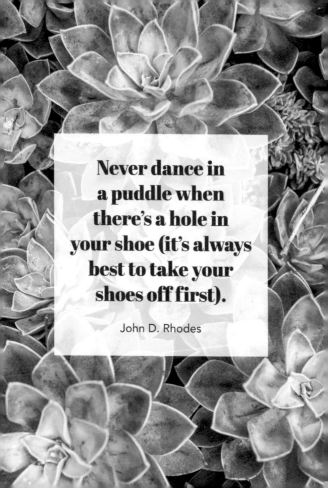

Never dance in
a puddle when
there's a hole in
your shoe (it's always
best to take your
shoes off first).

John D. Rhodes

PERFORM A
MAGIC TRICK.

SKIP EVERYWHERE, LEARN HOW TO SKATEBOARD OR ROLLER-SKATE, CHANGE YOUR HAIR COLOUR USING A WASHOUT DYE.

**EMBRACE YOUR
WEIRDNESS.**

Cara Delevingne

See how many marshmallows you can fit in your mouth.

DAYDREAM, *n.* A SERIES OF PLEASANT THOUGHTS THAT DISTRACT ONE'S ATTENTION FROM THE PRESENT.

LEARN TO WRITE YOUR NAME IN HIEROGLYPHICS.

THE BIGGEST ADVENTURE
YOU CAN EVER TAKE IS
TO LIVE THE LIFE OF
YOUR DREAMS.

Oprah Winfrey

INVENT YOUR OWN WORDS, SLIDE DOWN THE STAIRS IN A BLANKET OR SLEEPING BAG, MAKE ICE POPS, PAINT POTTERY, GO ON A MUDDY STROLL.

LEARN TO JUGGLE.

If people did not sometimes do silly things, nothing intelligent would ever get done.

LUDWIG WITTGENSTEIN

PLAN A
SCAVENGER
HUNT FOR
YOU AND
YOUR
FRIENDS.

ORGANIZE A GAME OF HIDE-AND-SEEK, WATCH A FAVOURITE **CHILDHOOD** MOVIE, BE YOUR FRIEND'S PERSONAL SHOPPER WHEN YOU NEXT HIT THE MALL.

OUTDREAM YOURSELF.

Pretend the floor is lava in your home.

Do anything,
but let it
produce joy.

Henry Miller

GO BEACHCOMBING,
LEARN TO SURF,
DECORATE WITH
FAIRY LIGHTS,
MAKE A DAISY CHAIN,
SPEND AN AFTERNOON
CHILLING
OUT IN A HAMMOCK.

UNLIKE ANY OTHER
FORM OF THOUGHT,
DAYDREAMING IS
ITS OWN REWARD.

Michael Pollan

LEARN TO BALLROOM DANCE.

GIVE NAMES
TO YOUR
MOST BELOVED
POSSESSIONS.

HAVE A WATER BALLOON FIGHT, GO BOATING ON A LAKE, VISIT A PLAYGROUND AND GO ON THE SWINGS AND SLIDES.

Change your accent for a day.

**Everything starts
as somebody's
daydream.**

Larry Niven

LET THE ADVENTURE BEGIN TODAY...

BUY A JAR AND FILL IT WITH COOKIES.

A SINGLE DREAM IS MORE POWERFUL THAN A THOUSAND REALITIES.

Nathaniel Hawthorne

SPEND A DAY CRAFTING, BINGE A TV SERIES, KNIT A PAIR OF SOCKS, READ SOMEONE'S PALM, DO A HANDSTAND.

I AM
ENDLESSLY
CREATING
MYSELF.

INVENT A NEW SPECIAL DAY THAT YOU AND YOUR FRIENDS CAN CELEBRATE.

HAVE YOUR
FRIENDS ROUND
FOR A "POSH"
AFTERNOON TEA.

I, for one,
live only
by and for
happiness.

David Vogel

BECOME A POET FOR A DAY.

GO TO A FUNFAIR MAKE A GIANT SANDCASTLE, DO SOME COLOURING IN.

The key to self-generated happiness (the only reliable kind) is the refusal to take oneself too seriously.

TOM ROBBINS

**CREATE A
MINIATURE
GARDEN IN
A SHOEBOX.**

WATCH YOUR FAVOURITE CHILDHOOD BAND OR SOLO ARTIST IN CONCERT.

PETRICHOR,
n. THE SMELL OF EARTH AFTER RAIN.

PAINT
BY NUMBERS,
WEAR AN OUTFIT
COMPRISED OF ONLY ONE
COLOUR,
EXPLORE WOODLAND
YOU'VE NEVER BEEN TO BEFORE,
TELL GHOST STORIES
WITH YOUR FRIENDS,
MAKE UP A DANCE.

THINK OF WHAT A PRECIOUS
PRIVILEGE IT IS TO BE ALIVE –
TO BREATHE. TO THINK.
TO ENJOY. TO LOVE.

Marcus Aurelius

Get creative and spend the afternoon painting patterns on pebbles.

MAKE YOUR OWN CORDIAL.

A day without laughter is a day wasted.

Nicolas Chamfort

CREATE

A QUIZ FOR YOUR FAMILY OR FRIENDS, MAKE A MIX TAPE, **DRAW** A SELF-PORTRAIT.

TRY YOUR HAND
AT CANDLE- OR
SOAP-MAKING
AND GIVE YOUR
CREATIONS
AS GIFTS TO
FRIENDS AND
FAMILY.

PLAY
BOARD
GAMES.

LIVE,

LAUGH,

LOVE.

IT'S KIND OF FUN
TO DO THE
IMPOSSIBLE.

Walt Disney

COOK THE MEAL YOU **LOVED MOST** AS A CHILD, CLIMB A HILL OR MOUNTAIN, GET UP EARLY TO WATCH THE SUNRISE, CREATE A SIGNATURE HANDSHAKE WITH A FRIEND, GO OUT IN A DOWNPOUR AND **ENJOY GETTING** SOAKED THROUGH.

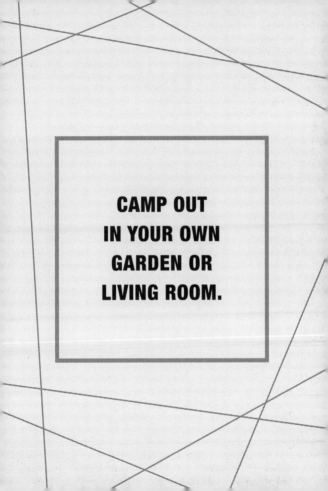

**CAMP OUT
IN YOUR OWN
GARDEN OR
LIVING ROOM.**

**If you obey
all the rules,
you miss all
the fun.**

Katharine Hepburn

Play "connect the dots" using all the moles on your arm.

WALK WITH A
SPRING
IN YOUR STEP,
SKIM STONES,
TELL SILLY JOKES.

Learn to play an instrument.

DREAM
BIG,
DREAM
OFTEN.

SOMETIMES. THE SIMPLE
THINGS ARE MORE FUN AND
MEANINGFUL THAN ALL THE
BANQUETS IN THE WORLD.

E. A. Bucchianeri

JOT DOWN THE
THINGS THAT
INTEREST OR
ENTERTAIN YOU
THROUGHOUT
THE DAY.

WRITE
A DICTIONARY OF YOUR FAVOURITE WORDS, COOK WITH INGREDIENTS YOU'VE NEVER USED BEFORE, GO ON A BIKE RIDE, AVOID WALKING ON THE CRACKS IN THE PAVEMENT.

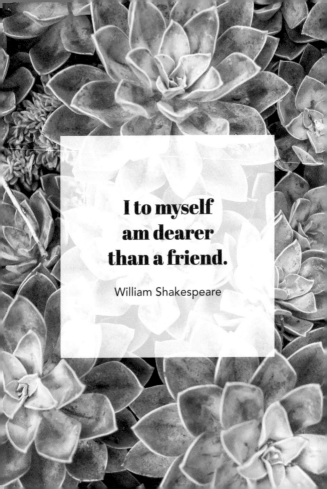

I to myself
am dearer
than a friend.

William Shakespeare

WRITE TO A
PEN PAL.

GAMBOL, *v.*
RUN OR JUMP
ABOUT PLAYFULLY.

DO CARTWHEELS AND HANDSTANDS.

SWAP CLOTHES WITH A
FRIEND,
TRY FLOWER-PRESSING,
SMILE
AT STRANGERS.

BE LED BY
THE DREAMS
IN YOUR HEART.

Roy T. Bennett

DO SOMETHING FUN OR CHALLENGING TO RAISE MONEY FOR A CHARITY CLOSE TO YOUR HEART.

I dream things that never were; and I say, "Why not?"

GEORGE BERNARD SHAW

Tie-dye an old, unwanted T-shirt.

WATCH A MUSICAL AND LEARN ONE OF THE SONGS BY HEART, **BECOME A** CHOCOLATIER FOR A DAY, THROW A BIRTHDAY PARTY FOR A PET, TAKE SILLY PHOTOS IN A **PHOTO BOOTH.**

LAZY SUNDAYS.

DELIGHT IN
WADING
THROUGH
FALLEN
LEAVES.

The future belongs
to those who believe
in the beauty of
their dreams.

Eleanor Roosevelt

MAKE
THE MOST
SPECTACULAR
DESSERT.

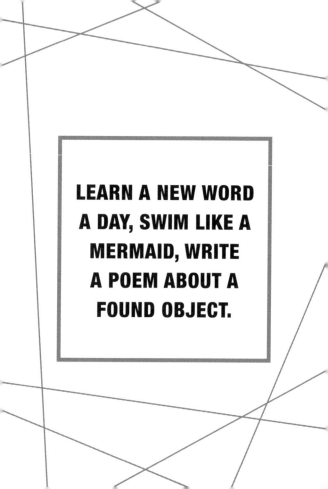

LEARN A NEW WORD
A DAY, SWIM LIKE A
MERMAID, WRITE
A POEM ABOUT A
FOUND OBJECT.

WE ARE SUCH
STUFF AS DREAMS
ARE MADE ON.

William Shakespeare

GET LOST IN WHAT YOU LOVE.

**GIVE YOURSELF
A DIFFERENT
COMPLIMENT
EVERY MORNING.**

TRY SINGING EVERYTHING YOU WANT TO SAY FOR A DAY.

ARRANGE A VIEWING AT A VERY
EXPENSIVE
HOUSE, GO BIRDWATCHING,
TRY MATCHMAKING,
CREATE YOUR OWN
SIGNATURE
DRINK, ORGANIZE
A "PARLOUR-GAME" EVENING.

Record
a funny
voicemail
greeting
message.

Never lose an opportunity of seeing anything beautiful.

Charles Kingsley

Without leaps of imagination, or dreaming, we lose the excitement of possibilities.

Gloria Steinem

**PLAN A DAY
OF FUN ACTIVITIES
WITH A FRIEND.**

WRITE MESSAGES IN THE SAND, FINISH SOMEONE'S SENTENCE BY SAYING "… ACCORDING TO THE PROPHECY", GO WAVE JUMPING.

HAVE A THUMB-WAR TOURNAMENT.

A DREAM IS
YOUR HEART
MAKING
A WISH.

**PERMIT YOUR DREAMS
TO SEE THE DAYLIGHT.**

Bernard Kelvin Clive

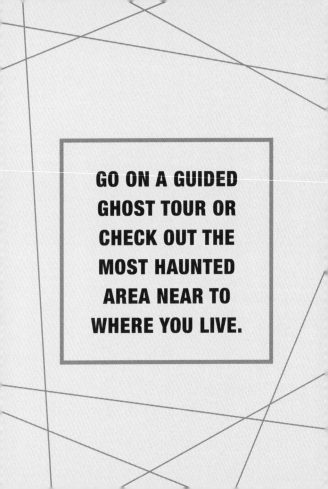

GO ON A GUIDED
GHOST TOUR OR
CHECK OUT THE
MOST HAUNTED
AREA NEAR TO
WHERE YOU LIVE.

You may tire
of reality but
you never tire
of dreams.

L. D. MONTGOMERY

CAST SOME GOOD-FORTUNE SPELLS, LEARN HOW TO **MOONWALK**, ATTEND A CRAFT FAIR, HAVE A LONG, CANDLELIT **BUBBLE BATH**, SPIN ON THE SPOT UNTIL **YOU FEEL DIZZY.**

GO TO A
RESTAURANT
AND BECOME
A FOOD
CRITIC FOR
THE EVENING.

FOLLOW YOUR DREAMS; THEY KNOW THE WAY.

MAKE YOUR OWN SIGNATURE TEA.

MAKE SOME FUNKY
JEWELLERY,
BAKE CUPCAKES,
RELAX
UNDER A TREE
ON A WARM DAY.

DREAMS ARE
NECESSARY
TO LIFE.

Anaïs Nin

Wear a ridiculously bright outfit to work.

I dream. Sometimes
I think it's the only
right thing to do.

Haruki Murakami

PLAY
CHARADES.

GO WITH ME.
SOMEWHERE.
ANYWHERE.

ORGANIZE A SPORTS DAY WITH

FRIENDS,

ASK A LOVED ONE FOR A

MASSAGE,

LISTEN TO BIRDSONG,

GO ON A HIKE,

BECOME A DOG WALKER.

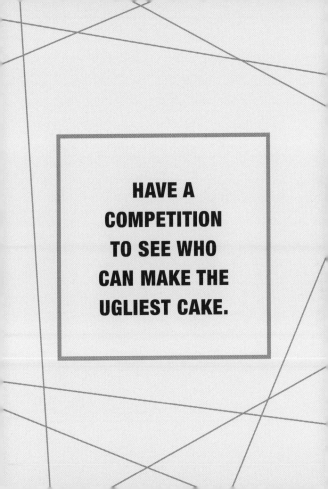

HAVE A
COMPETITION
TO SEE WHO
CAN MAKE THE
UGLIEST CAKE.

DREAMS, IF THEY'RE
ANY GOOD, ARE
ALWAYS A LITTLE
BIT CRAZY.

Ray Charles

PULL A
FUNNY FACE
EVERY TIME
YOU SEE
YOUR OWN
REFLECTION.

MAKE A DREAMCATCHER,
LEARN THE
TAROT,
MAKE A HUMAN
PYRAMID.

EVERY DAY BRINGS A
CHANCE FOR YOU TO
DRAW IN A BREATH,
KICK OFF YOUR SHOES,
AND DANCE.

Oprah Winfrey

Grow your own herbs and vegetables.

HALCYON, *a.*
PERIOD OF TIME
IN THE PAST THAT
WAS IDYLLICALLY
HAPPY AND
PEACEFUL.

GO CAROLLING IN THE HEIGHT OF SUMMER.

LISTEN TO WHALE MUSIC,
DOODLE
SOMETHING WITH
YOUR EYES CLOSED,
HAVE A PROPER
BELLY LAUGH,
MAKE SNOW
ANGELS,
BUILD AN ELASTIC-BAND BALL.

We must dare,
and dare again,
and go on daring.

Georges Jacques Danton

MAKE YOUR HOME
AN URBAN JUNGLE
BY FILLING IT
WITH PLANTS.

Fortune favours the brave.

Virgil

ONLY THE CURIOUS HAVE ADVENTURES.

DECK YOUR HOUSE OR GARDEN OUT IN THE MOST RIDICULOUS CHRISTMAS DECORATIONS WHEN IT'S NOT EVEN CHRISTMAS, MAKE MATCHING BRACELETS FOR YOU AND YOUR FRIENDS, START COLLECTING SOMETHING: UNUSUAL COINS, UGLY SHOES OR PEBBLES.

GO
GEOCACHING.

GO WILD SWIMMING.

IN MY DREAMS,
I NEVER HAVE
AN AGE.

Madeleine L'Engle

FIND OUT IF
YOU SLEEP TALK –
RECORD YOURSELF
ON YOUR PHONE.

LEARN CALLIGRAPHY,
GO TO A QUIET PLACE
AND MAKE AS MUCH

NOISE

AS YOU LIKE, START
OR JOIN A BOOK CLUB,
EAT JELLY AND
ICE CREAM,
MAKE BATH BOMBS.

A daily dose of daydreaming heals the heart, soothes the soul, and strengthens the imagination.

Richelle E. Goodrich

Start a blog about something that interests you.

DREAMS ARE
IDEAS WITH
WINGS.

LEARN A NEW FACT ABOUT THE UNIVERSE.

DREAM

EVERY DAY.

Don't Quit Your Daydream.

If you're interested in finding out more about our books, find us on Facebook at **Summersdale Publishers** and follow us on Twitter at @**Summersdale**.

www.summersdale.com

IMAGE CREDITS

pp.3, 4, 25, 44, 75, 99, 129, 151, 159
© koTRA/Shutterstock.com

pp.7, 54, 83, 109, 136
© Elena Sherengovskaya/Shutterstock.com

pp.8, 16, 22, 36, 38, 46, 56, 66, 71, 85, 95, 100, 108, 110, 117, 122, 135, 145, 153 © Millay/Shutterstock.com

pp.10, 32, 59, 86, 114, 146
© Nadine Spires/Shutterstock.com

pp.15, 40, 62, 91, 121, 139
© Love the wind/Shutterstock.com

pp.17, 36, 67, 94, 116, 144 © runLenarun/Shutterstock.com

pp.27, 52, 78, 106, 131, 154
© Zamurovic Photography/Shutterstock.com